Palewε.

Inside the Blue House

Poems by Sonia Jarema

Inside the Blue House

First edition 2019 from Palewell Press,
www.palewellpress.co.uk

Printed and bound in the UK

ISBN 978-1-911587-16-3

A CIP catalogue record for this title is available from the
British Library.

Inside the Blue House

Acknowledgements

Acknowledgements are due to the following on-line and print publications in which some of these poems or earlier versions first appeared: *The Barnet poetry anthology 2014*, *Envoi*, *The Interpreter's House, LitWorld 2, The North*, *South* and *Stand*.

I would also like to thank Enfield Poets, Forest Poets, Katherine Gallagher, Myra Schneider and Mimi Khalvati for their tutorage and support.

I would also like to thank my long-suffering friends who have given me feedback on poems, performances and kept me going with words of criticism and encouragement.

Thanks to my mum and dad and sister Halyna. And to my cousins in Ukraine.

Last but not least thanks to Lou, Ivan and Arianna, my family, without whom I would never have written these poems.

Для мами і тата

For Mum and Dad

Contents

My family history

My mum was born in a village near Lesko town in South East Poland in 1934 or 1935 or 1936. Officially she was born in 1932 but as she had no birth certificate, she added on some years to reduce the age gap between her and my dad who was born in 1921. She was ethnically Ukrainian. Her grandmother was very strict and didn't believe in girls going to school so my mum never learnt to read or write. She told me that when she was 12 years old all Ukrainians were ordered to pack up and leave (I assume as part of Operation Vistula). They were put on cattle trucks and didn't know where they were being sent. After a long arduous journey, with nowhere to go to the toilet and only the food they'd taken with them, my mum, her two brothers (one of whom was deaf), her mother and her grandmother arrived in Olztyn. They had been forced to start a new life in what had been Prussia and was now part of Poland.

Her next relocation was to be of her own choice. She wanted a different life not one tied to working the land. Her distant cousin had already settled in Britain and married a Ukrainian living in Bedford. They were friends with my dad who was himself looking for a wife and at their suggestion my dad wrote to my mum. She replied – well that's what my dad thought at the time but in fact it was my mum's friend who wrote the letters. They carried on 'writing' until he invited her over in 1965. She was surprised to find that he'd lost most of the beautiful hair he'd had in the photo he'd sent her, and I imagine he was surprised to find that she couldn't read or write. She found work sewing buttons on coats for Eastex until she was replaced by a machine. My mum never learnt to speak English and never went back to either Ukraine or Poland. She had an unusual sense of humour and was a very loving mum. When I was 5 years old she was diagnosed with schizophrenia and the medications available at that time made life hard for her.

My dad was one of three boys, his mum would line them up in a production line to help make vareniki – the little Ukrainian dumplings.

He was born in Nove Selo not far from Lviv or, as it was called at that time, Lvov. Both my parents were from the historical area of Galicia that both Poles and Ukrainians laid claim to. Nove Selo experienced similar evacuations to my mum's place of birth but in reverse – the Poles were forced out as the area switched from Polish to Soviet hands. Things were slightly more complicated for my dad as his mother was Polish and his dad was a strongly patriotic Ukrainian. My grandmother Antonina overheard plans to force out all the Poles and burn their houses down. In the dead of night, she ran to her family and told them to pack up and leave as soon as possible which they did. Antonina loved her husband deeply so she stayed.

The oldest boy, Basil, was taken into the Red Army in the Second World War and never returned but wasn't reported as dead. His daughters still to this day don't know what became of him. Michael, the youngest, was kidnapped twice by the Germans for forced labour. Each time he managed to escape only to be sent for 14 years hard labour to Satka in Siberia, along with his parents, as punishment for being a coachman driving a horse and cart for Ukrainian freedom fighters. My dad, the middle son, was taken to Germany in 1941, returning home very briefly in 1943. After the war there was an attempt to repatriate the displaced persons from the camps in Germany. The first Ukrainians that were sent back to the USSR (Union of Soviet Socialist Republics) were killed or sent to the gulags so naturally the remaining ones did not want to return home. The United Kingdom agreed to accept 86,000 displaced persons and my dad was sent to England on the understanding that he work in one of the industries with labour shortages, for a minimum of 3 years. He chose agriculture and, along with 140 other Ukrainians, ended up living in an ex-prisoner of war camp in Newgate Street village, Hertfordshire. From there they were taken to work in the local glass houses growing roses, cucumbers and tomatoes. In 1946 the Ukrainians had set up the AUGB (Association of Ukrainians in Great Britain) with their headquarters in Holland Park and a network of clubs all over Britain providing a support network for those far away from home.

He didn't contact his family back home for years as he feared it would have a negative impact on them. The Soviets frowned upon anyone with relatives on the other side of the Iron Curtain. Ukrainians didn't dare return home for decades, as to have left the USSR even against your will was a crime punishable by death or the Siberian prison camps. My dad sent a parcel of dress material for his nieces at first anonymously and he started to exchange letters regularly with his brother but they were censored.

My parents settled in Luton where my dad was employed on the production line at Vauxhall Motors. Here he was called Joe as all foreigners were. Once my dad and uncle did try to speak by phone. Uncle travelled to relations in Poland and my dad waited at a phone box at an appointed time and I remember my dad saying, 'Hello this is Ivan from England', and then telling me the line had gone dead.

In 1981 he was determined to go back home to visit and applied for a passport. By the time it arrived he had died suddenly of a heart attack leaving my mum, myself aged 13 and my sister aged 11. Finally, in 1999 my sister and I went to Ukraine for the first time; it was like coming home. What struck me on that first visit were the massive statues to poets – Shevchenko and Franko. Literature had been so vital in keeping the Ukrainian identity alive. Uncle was so pleased to see his brother's daughters and we were happy to have found our family whom we visit regularly.

Some of the names here and in the poems have been changed as a mark of respect to the people who were kind enough to share their stories with me.

A very brief history of Ukraine

Ukraine's beginnings are to be found in Kievan Rus', a city-state originating in the 9th century that was very powerful until its sacking by the Mongols in the mid-14th century. Ukrainian identity survived Mongol, Polish, Habsburg and Russian rule but it wasn't until the 20th century that the country gained independence—briefly in 1918, after the fall of the Russian Empire, and then from 1991 with the collapse of the USSR.

In the early 1920s, after the demise of the Habsburg Empire, Ukraine was split between Poland and a new Ukrainian Soviet Socialist Republic. Initially the Soviet Union encouraged Ukrainian culture but soon implemented policies with devastating effects. The purges of the 1920s and 30s resulted in approximately 80% of the Ukrainian intelligentsia losing their lives, fleeing or being exiled. Furthermore in 1932 Stalin enforced strict grain requisitions resulting in an artificial famine known as the Holodomor which killed at least 3 million people in Ukraine alone.

During the Second World War Ukraine suffered greatly at the hands of both Hitler and Stalin. Ukrainians either fought for the Red Army or were recruited/taken by the Germans for largely unpaid/slave labour. Many others joined Ukrainian partisan groups fighting for independence. After the war, Ukraine's border was redrawn; what ensued was the killing of ordinary people both Polish and Ukrainian who happened to be too close to or on the wrong side of the line.

Ukraine gained independence peacefully in 1991. Both the Orange Revolution in 2004 and Euromaidan in 2014 were attempts to shake off lingering ties with Russia as well as being shows of dissatisfaction with corruption in Ukraine. In February 2014, President Yanukovych, who had strong ties to Putin, was overthrown. Putin reacted by invading the Crimea, then Eastern Ukraine and more recently seizing Ukrainian vessels and servicemen in the Azov sea. We wait anxiously to see how this chapter will unfold.

Apologies for any inaccuracies in this attempt to condense the history of Ukraine. For further reading please refer to the bibliography at the back of the pamphlet.

Sonia Jarema December 2018

Inside the Blue House

Nove Selo, Ukraine 1999

Lightning strikes the conversation,
jolting Uncle to the television.
His long face scythes the semi-darkness
as he says nothing is earthed here.

Hrym hrymet padaie doschch.*
The rain falls in Ukrainian. As a child
all words fell in Ukrainian. Now,
as in the dubbed 'Columbo',

few original words remain.
'*Rodyna vsi razo*',** says Uncle.
Then he fixes me with deep blue eyes
undiminished by the dusk

and my questions file from his mouth.
When I shake my head, he cocks his
and smiles as though a joke
had been whispered in his ear.

* Thunder thunders rain falls

**Reunited

Homecoming

We walk into the dark
of the waiting room
and make faces out of silhouettes.
Cousin Lesia presses flowers
into our hands and then the potholed road
takes us to a line of relatives.

More family than we've ever had
around us pass us black bread,
kovbasa, Russian salad, roe, *sopoka*
and boiled eggs with deep sunshine
yolks sprinkled with paprika
and freshly grated horseradish.

Then Lesia brings soup,
followed by *vareniki* and *holopchi*
and finally cakes: *sernik* and *makivnek*.
Speeches and shots of vodka
punctuate the evening.

At the spot that held the house
where our dad was born,
his brother tells my sister,
'You have his laugh.'
Between the apple orchard and
the sweetcorn field an old man

stops to ask our name and says,
'Your dad was a good man.'
In the closet Uncle rummages the past
and finds the letter he hadn't wanted
to believe. A decade in Siberia
and he's the only brother left.

Pan Osadchiuk

Pan Osadchiuk's eyes brim and his hands shake.
I ask him about the past but instead
he tells me about the tablets he takes
for his nerves. The water holds in his eyes
and he says, 'We have three cats now,
they eat dinner at the table with us
wearing napkins round their necks. Come see how
I've trained them to use knives and forks.'

Playing the game

Mr Lenciv's at the door looking
beaten, telling me, 'Your dad's
collapsed.' He's always telling
jokes. I close the door on him.

But then the policeman comes,
says he'll take Mama to Dad.
For the first time, my sister and I
are at home without parents.

I beat time against the table leg;
she opens the writing desk and brings
the map to me. Some of its creases
are torn. We make a game of anything,

taking turns at night to make prams
with our legs. I let her rant how when
our dad comes home she'll break
his cigarettes to stop him smoking.

I let her talk but my foot stops
keeping beat and I think,
'He's dead.' We play
the street name game to stop

the silence from growing bigger than us.
We fight it, making time elastic until
Mama comes back with a bag
of his cut clothes that smell of hospital.

They'd got a Polish woman to translate.
Mama howls and weeps. We've never seen
her cry before. 'But you never loved him,'
I say and she calls me Satan.

I sleep with her that night, holding
my breath when I can't catch hers
and watch bold car headlights
sweep across the ceiling, missing me.

Dinner time

For Halyna

Mama feeds us as though we have a field to plough.
Eating is slow, so much gets caught in my throat.

My sister plays the role of cookery presenter
and presses her fork into the curved backs

of the potatoes, mashing then flattening them into a circle
as she explains each stage to her audience.

I'm not the audience – I'm on her side of the screen.
She turns over her fork and picks out two circles before

turning it back to scrape a curve, 'And now,'
she says, 'you have a smiley face.'

the earth holds secrets

tell me, tell me

                your mother's hair is blonde

no it is raven

                you never knew her before the darkness took her

she is light and dark – her beauty dappled

                but you never saw her before

whoever gets to see before?

                reach back for her words, let the images delineate,

tell me, does she stand on the bend of a river, hair streaming down?

                her tears flow, as she throws goodbyes to the surge of the river San

her face is a golden sun

                she watches neighbours torch their houses goodbye

the blind train carries them north

                only the river is never swept away

Desire isn't where I left it

The Dart carried the sun
      on its back, over
smooth rocks,
      to splinter on the weir.
On the other side
      it did come back together –
didn't it? Not like this
      river in Ukraine
whose course
      the villagers changed,
leaving this stretch
      stagnating with patience.
The grass moves
      and frogs take
massive leaps into
      the darkest water.

Blood song

For R.S.

Sitting by you I can feel the pull
of the underground river sucking stones,
sending your syllables chattering
into the music of my other tongue.

The rhythm of your voice takes me
to the edge of my father's village.
It creaks open the cemetery gate,
leads me past wrought iron crosses

to gaze at the land that springs
with forests and crests with geese.
The blood songs under our skin
unearth their own kith and kin.

Mariyka's song

The village is a ghost of itself,
more people are dying than being born.

It's been so long since Mariyka sang.
But now, by the lake in her sister's garden,

she offers lines of a Ukrainian song
I don't know. I'm tone-deaf in English

but her voice is still strong enough to pull mine
in her undertow. She says something like:

'Young one, see how you draw after me';
she smiles and we start the line again.

55 Douglas Road

After 'Leaving' by Katherine Gallagher

Nadia sits in her fake fur,
hunched like a vulture.
Fine bone china cups
rattle open-mouthed
back onto their saucers.

Tea cups filled, emptied,
washed, filled, emptied.
There's not enough china
for one sitting. The house
bulges with the conversations

that loosen with the black ties.
Sandwiches and cake
whipped in and down
and all the while
we stand like children.

Then you ask, 'But where
are the grownups?'
'We are the grownups',
I say as the crockery
starts to break in on itself.

Strawberry cheesecake

Mama starts rocking, her lips moving faster
        as if she's shivering but she isn't. My sister
sits, pulling apart her split ends, miles away.
        Mama's hair looks like she's been under water
but it's darkened with grease. Her legs are red
        from the gas fire hissing hot air into the room.

Mama hasn't washed, fed us or left the room.
        She tells us 'Veleke Pan is coming faster
than you think. The Big Man will wear red
        when he comes to take you away.' My sister
looks up and Mama's eyes start to water,
        'Big Man from Doncaster will take you away.'

We watch Baby Jane, her colour's bled away,
        Mama gets up and paces the back room.
Next it's horse racing; our blood turns to water
        at every mention of Doncaster. Faster
than my choice, the jockey in red my sister
        picked races home. She always picks red.

In the freezer we find a cheesecake, 'It's red,
        don't eat it.' 'We won't', we steal it away
to defrost in the front room. My sister
        hacks at it, making a mess in the room.
Our cheeks raise peaks as we eat faster
        and faster, spluttering laughter until water

fills my mouth. Nausea pushes through the water,
     my stomach heaves and my hands can't hold the red.
It spills over onto the carpet, bringing Mama faster
     than we've ever seen her move. 'He'll take you away',
she smiles with that knowing look before pacing the room.
     'The police won't let him', says my sister.

The knocker cracks down on the door, my sister
     rushes to the sink, grabs the knife lying in water.
Mama says, 'Come back into the back room.'
     A shape looms through the glass; my sister's face turns red.
I pull her back into the room, willing him to go away
     but the knocker knocks louder and faster.

Behind my sister's back the knife drips water.
     She won't stay in the back room; my heart beats faster
as Mama says, 'Red brings the devil to take you away.'

The red broom

The red broom swept my children away.
In my neighbour Marysia's kitchen,
I saw their fingers rising in aspic.
'No, you've lost your mind to grief', she said.
'Marysia, a mother knows her children's hands.'

A mother knows her children's hands.
Grief claws its fingers through my hair.
It pulls and tears at my scalp.
I lose my mind to grief.

Now in this foreign land,
my precious children, I can't eat.
Why does this hospital milk taste so sour?
In your innocence you can't understand,
if I eat, then it's you I eat.

Roses

As I sit hunched in the outgrown swing,
lank, dun-coloured hair swings
into my eyes and you say, 'Sit up straight;
don't be embarrassed by your figure.'

I draw my shoulders closer together
and hide the breasts that had suddenly
pushed their way through my chest,
one night while I was sleeping.

You turn the earth over and cut
my playground from under me.
'I think roses here. What do you think?'
Be quiet. I'm trying to hate you.

                    **

I kiss your beeswax-coloured forehead.
You are smiling; you will never
speak again. I shuffle my feet and point out
that your date of birth on the lid is wrong.

Your coat and tweed cap still hang
in the hallway. We think that
you might return as suddenly as you left,
bringing in the smell of rain-drenched earth.

No return

The eyes of the train are open.
                I want everything and nothing.
Keep your line, keep your banks,

don't clasp the river. I am not crying for you.
                I am crying for my father.
Hearts can cry and strength can bleed away.

His heart tore its throat with longing.
                Where does all this sadness come from?
It comes from trying to go back

                to where we stood and being
struck dumb, again and again.

Market day

She held her grandson's hand
and strode him through
the rapidly emptying market

as though purpose and speed
could get them safely home.
She held his hand as though

she held his life. She held his hand
and when the moment came
that life left him, she held on.

My uncle told me

one man in the village
was so scared of the Russians
that he took every memento
of his brother and threw each one
onto the fire lest the Communists
punish him for having a relation
the other side of the Iron Curtain.

Now he has no living brother
and nothing to show
he was here.

.

Bela Bartok's Violin Sonata BB 124 1

The violin shouted, whispered, implored;
it did everything I thought it couldn't
so I listened and saw the places I could go
without moving, without forever striving
and knew that however much I wanted
to cry for you it wouldn't bring you
any closer than you already are.

Ukrainian rye

On the porch of my cousin's house
I show my son, daughter, and nephew
the magic of Ukrainian bread which stops
the blood flowing from a cut in my lip.

Quickly bored, they scatter like chickens
to play on a mound of white sand
overlooked by the church which stands
on land donated by my grandfather.

The priest meets me by the garden fence
with a traditional greeting. I can't recall
the expected response so I mumble in reply.
Later, when I tell my cousin, she says

'You should have said...'as we pass a man
scything grass and she hails him with,
'God grant you luck.' He wishes us the same in air
that has carried these greetings for centuries.

Arianna

It's the stalks the mower missed
that cut into the picture. You in a

ripped t-shirt and legs smeared with dirt.
Your hair fuzzy with yesterday's plaits

like someone from my childhood.
You shake your head when a boy

offers to push you on the tyre-swing,
wanting me instead. The boy talks

to everyone. He has a hint of a language
he never possessed. Tucking air

under his arm, he shows how he can
lift his classmate clear off the ground.

He runs away and I go back to my patch
of shade, watch you climb a wall

and wave each time you stop.

Flying lessons

A man with a cut-throat scar offers
        peanuts to children and adults gathered
under the trees in Kensington Gardens.

He shows them how to hold out their arms
        as if they could fly and to cup their hands
ever so slightly. A woman flings open

her arms. 'You look like you are about to be crucified!'
        cracks the short, stout man by her side.
The parakeets won't land on her and, amongst leaves, still

fresh and tender green, it's hard to make them out.
        When they eat from our hands their red eyes are cold.
Their leaving's like a breaking apart of the tree.

Have those words cost you anything?

Do you know how they will be turned
this way and that to catch the light
where it wasn't meant to fall
and bring darkness that wasn't intended?
The limestone walls weep when it rains.

Son and daughter turn in bed like the fish
we'd seen trapped in a rock pool.
Fishes lit green as they rushed
to the opening only to turn suddenly
and darken at the too narrow outlet.

Touch paper

The sun low in the sky, Mama soft in the light,
turning to take the small cloth sack of flour,
dust and millet Danylko swept from the attic floor.
He sits down on the wooden bench
with a back so well-worn that he can only make out
the ghost of a tree. A lone ant plots a course
across his thigh. He brings down the pad of
his middle finger and licks it off quickly,
eyes heavy with shame. Mama pours the flour
into a bowl, chops up the blanched nettles
that looked like deep green leeches and scatters them in.
Then using the smallest cup they have,
she scoops it into bucket of water. She shakes
a few drops at a time as she works the mixture.

He calls this making rain. Rain is some kind of magic
that makes things change. Life is a different pace
and a different volume now. Each week it seems
the volume is being turned down a level.
Sometimes he has to run, cover his ears and shout
to stop himself feeling he is being buried alive.
If Mama hears him she'll grab his arm and in her new voice rasp,
'What's wrong with you – has the devil got inside of you?'

Mama smiles as she pulls the dough
into two pieces, shaping each into an oval.
Short green veins run under the skin.
He waits patiently, careful not to swing his legs.
Mama passes him a stick and a small screw
of newspaper. Her smile has already gone.
He slips off the bench, spears the paper onto the stick
and opens the metal door of the white brick oven,
holding himself back as the hot air rushes out.
He pushes the end of the stick inside to the top.
The paper blackens but doesn't catch fire.
With a shove Mama sends the bread on its way.

Kyiv 1999

The light from the bathroom glows pink;
on pushing the door open we find red roses,
in the bath, sipping the water's surface.

My sister fetches the stout woman who sits
by the lift at a wide table. Keys jump
at her waist as she shouts to the maids

to bring vases. They work quickly as the stems drip
like babies lifted out of baths.
Outside the hotel a *babu'sya* begs

and on the next street yet another then another.
Speakers high on lamp posts blast out
pop songs to empty streets. We run

skimming colour across the grey landscape
until we reach a square lit up by Saint Sophia's
blue, white and gold. The centuries

have locked away her medieval heart.
Lonely in her beauty, we leave her until
finally we find a square full of life.

People singing Ukrainian folk and pop
around a fountain; their voices lift the stifling silence.
Later, framed by a metal rainbow,

two giant silver figures stand holding
a medal, the Order of Friendship.
Kyiv lies below sliced by the river Dnipro.

Ukraine you come to me in dreams.

Отче Наш, the Lord's Prayer,
flows from my lips. There are eyes on me
that slide as soon as I turn my head.

I take my friend to a funeral and watch
as a detached blue and yellow car bonnet
is carried into church. Its edges

are shaped like Ukraine's borders
but one part is missing. A tryzyb,
Ukraine's three-toothed national symbol,

is drawn on the bonnet – it has lost
a tooth. Inside the church people stand
and drink as blood ebbs from their feet.

Talk about the weather

'Seems to have its own weather here.'
Sloped banks carry snowdrops higher.
'Lots of times I've seen the rain move across
the field the other side of the brook
while this place stays dry.' If I hold myself
in this place nothing will fracture. I know
it's a lie, everything is already falling apart.

What the silver birches know

Volod eases my sister's case
over the kerb. His voice rushes
like a bell rope till it catches

and the words ring out, 'I want
your children to visit mine.'
By the road, silver-flanks of birches

glow against the dark loam.
We pass a church, outside of which
people wait holding vessels

to fill with holy water. Not wanting
to pour out our drinking water, we tell
Volod we have no empty bottles.

The path stretches on to the airport.
The silver birches know we'll return
to hear their breathless stories.

The last Ukis

Outside the church my sister scans
for Ukrainian faces as we wait for the hearse.
Two old ladies walk past and in one I see a hint
of a once familiar face. I try her name
and she comes over; I tell her we are

the Yarema girls. She looks at us as if
she's flicking through the pages of our lives
and then nods a deeply drawn smile,
happy how she's found us. She turns to
my brother-in- law, holds his arm and says,

'I remember you, you're English –
they're good people', then switches
to Ukrainian, 'I said it right didn't I?'
Her voice slows, 'I'm old. Now there are
only two Ukrainians left in Bedford.'

The service is in English. I miss
the swelling and falling away
of the Ukrainian. The priest reads the eulogy,
how 'Uncle' loved school so much
not even the weather could stop him –

strapping on skis he'd fly through the snow.
But the Germans stopped him, kidnapped him
for forced labour at the age of 14, though
he was one of the lucky ones – sent to a farm
where the family were kind.

Our father never spoke
of his time in Germany, not to us,
not to anyone. When liberated by the British,
'Uncle' was allowed to come to England if he chose
to work in agriculture, mining or the mills.

He chose the countryside, later moved
onto the brick-works. Men of
different nationalities came together
in the heat of the kilns to make London bricks
and they are gathered here now.

As the priest invites us to say
our final goodbyes the old lady is unfolding
a plastic bag. Once she's settled whatever it is
she wants to settle inside, she stands in the aisle.
Her coat remembers her stoutness.

Pain twists her face like a match catching light.
Then she kisses the coffin next to the cross
of blue and yellow roses before making
her farewells. Refusing a lift, she sets off
to the bus stop back to her husband in hospital.

The watchers

We are the lowest of the low.
We watch, we record and we don't
intervene. We watch, we record,
we don't turn away. We can't
block our noses, close our eyes
or cover our ears. We are open
doors to storming troops. We are
defenceless against blows,
we are the bruises that show
the silent violence. We are always
too late or too soon. We are
the warning cries no-one wants
to hear. We are wanting.

Further reading / Bibliography

Books:

Applebaum, Anne *Gulag: A History* (New York: Doubleday, 2003)

Applebaum, Anne *Red Famine* (London: Allen Lane, 2017)

Dimarov, Anatoliy, trans. Franko,Roma *A Hunger Most Cruel: The Human Face of the 1932-1933 Terror-Famine in Soviet Ukraine* (Winnipeg: Language Lanterns Publication, 2002)

Grossman, Vasilii *Everything flows* (New York: New York Classic books, 2009)

Magocsi, Paul Robert *A History of Ukraine* (Toronto: University of Toronto Press,1996)

Samchuk, Ulas. trans Franko, Roma *Maria* (Winnipeg: Language Lanterns Publication, 2011)

Snyder, Timothy, *Bloodlands* (London: Vintage, 2015)

Subtelny, Orest, *Ukraine: A History* (Toronto: University of Toronto Press, 1994)

Wilson, Andrew *The Ukrainians: unexpected nation* (New Haven: Yale University Press, 2000)

Websites – accounts of the famine:

https://www.garethjones.org/press_diaries.htm

http://www.holodomorsurvivors.ca/Survivors2.html

Sonia Jarema - Biography

Sonia Jarema is a poet, writer, learning support assistant, self-employed gardener and mother of two. She was born in Luton, to Ukrainian parents. Her dad worked on the production line at Vauxhall Motors and her mum sewed buttons on coats for Eastex. Most people had never heard of Ukraine and even though the country has now been featured in the news people still ask her if Ukrainian is the same language as Russian. As a child she had to memorise and recite Ukrainian poetry and either this started or fed her love of language and its inner music. When she started school she couldn't speak English but gradually it took over as her main language. Her poems have been published in Stand, The North, South Bank Poetry, South, Envoi, LitWorld 2 and The Interpreter's House as well as on-line and in several anthologies. Her novel was longlisted for the Penguin WriteNow programme in 2016-2017.

Ukrainian history wasn't taught at school so it was left to the second generation to carry it. In her poetry she explores this history alongside the breaking apart and coming back together of a family. She writes because stories and words gave her oxygen when life grew difficult. She writes to explore the intense pictures that were fixed in her memory when words failed her. Writing for her is a way of processing experiences that have no place in everyday conversation. It's a way of drawing people into another person's loneliness as well as combating it. She writes to cling on to what is being lost, to catch histories before they slip away unrecorded. She writes for people no longer here, to show that they were here. She writes because she has to and without it she's lost.

Palewell Press

Palewell Press is an independent publisher handling poetry, fiction and non-fiction with a focus on books that foster Justice, Equality and Sustainability.
The Editor can be reached on enquiries@palewellpress.co.uk